The Monarch Butterfly

BY

CELESTINE ROBERTS

Table of Contents

Introduction

The Monarch Butterfly (Denaus plaxippus) is one of the most widely recognised butterflies there is. Its characteristic orange and black webbed wings with white dots make it also one of the most beautiful.

This book will help you familiarise yourself with the Monarch Butterfly and it's amazing life-cycle. Later in the book there are some very useful tips for creating a Monarch habitat in your own back garden, including the conditions that will help to attract butterflies and the types of plants they need to feed on. For the true Monarch enthusiast, there is even a section on raising butterflies which is a fascinating and rewarding process. We hope you enjoy reading about this beautiful creature!

What makes the Monarch butterfly so special?

There are lots of things that make the Monarch special, apart from its beautiful appearance. For example, you might be surprised to know that the Monarch is poisonous in its larval stage. This is because the butterflies lay their eggs on poisonous milkweed plants. When the eggs hatch and the larvae emerge, they eat the milkweed, and this makes them poisonous to predators. This is why the Monarch is also known as a "milkweed butterfly". Once the caterpillars turn in to butterflies, they no longer eat the milkweed. Instead, they like to eat nectar from flowers, sip water and even eat certain minerals in the soil.

Another thing that sets the Monarch Butterfly apart is its impressive migration patterns. Every year, these delicate creatures travel huge distances. They spend the winters in Mexico and Southern California and when the weather begins to get warmer, they travel north to Canada, only to return to Mexico again when the winter comes around once more. Of course, North America and Mexico aren't the only places where the Monarch can be seen. It has also been found in places as far flung as Australasia, the United Kingdom, Western Europe and the Canary Islands. However, only the butterflies living in the Americas make such a huge migration.

Monarch Butterfly Biology

The Monarch Butterfly is cold blooded, and relies on the sun to keep it warm. This is why these butterflies make such a huge annual pilgrimage to warmer climates - in the cold they would simply die. Here are some other important aspects of the Monarch's biology that you should know about.

Eggs

The Monarch's eggs are tiny, white and can often be found stuck to the underside of milkweed leaves. They have tiny ridges running the length of the shell. Under a microscope, you will see that there are tiny holes in the top of each egg - this is how the eggs are fertilized when the butterflies mate. More often than not, there will be one egg per milkweed plant; a good way to provide plenty of food for each hatchling! The widest part of the egg will be attached firmly to the leaf, with the egg itself being surprisingly solid, helping to protect the larvae inside. A wax-like substance inside the shell prevents it from drying out, keeping it relatively flexible so that the larvae can grow big enough to hatch. When this happens, the newly formed caterpillar will chew its way out of the egg from the top end.

Caterpillar

Caterpillars are tiny eating machines, and can be very fast at polishing off a milkweed plant! Their bodies are comprised of a head, thorax and abdomen. Caterpillars have short antennae-like structures on their heads and rear ends, as well as a pair of jaws which they use to chew. The antennae or tentacles and another structure called the maxillary palp (a bump located under the mouth) help them to find food. You might be surprised to learn that the caterpillar has not one but six pairs of simple eyes, called ocelli. However, despite having several eyes, these creatures have quite poor vision and still rely heavily on their other sensory organs to find food.

The caterpillar's body is divided into segments, each with a pair of legs. Some of these legs are actually "false" legs or prolegs, which have small hooks on them that help the caterpillar to attach itself to leaves. Another curious fact about these creatures is that they have tiny holes in the sides of their abdomen and thorax which are called spiracles. These holes obtain oxygen and deliver it to the body, using long tubes called tracheae.

Pupa

The Monarch larva or caterpillar goes through a stage called pupation, which is the transformation it goes through to become a butterfly. At the beginning of this process, the caterpillar splits its exoskeleton (a skeleton on the outside of the body, which is common to a lot of insects) and begins to shed its skin by literally wriggling out of it. Next, a spiney structure called the cremaster is exposed at the end of the caterpillar's body, and this is used to hook on to a ready-made silk pad that the caterpillar has already woven onto the leaf. The cremaster and the silk pad keep the pupa anchored to the leaf while it undergoes its miraculous transformation into a butterfly.

Butterfly (adult)

The butterfly's body is made up of a head, thorax, abdomen and of course, those beautiful wings! If you look closer though, you'll see these creatures have a few hidden features which nature has bestowed on them. For example, a straw-like proboscis acts as the butterfly's tongue, and is used to suck up the nectar during feeding. When the butterfly isn't using its built-in straw, it simply curls it up out of the way. There are six legs, but it often looks like there are only four of them, because one pair of legs is often curled up close to the thorax. The interesting thing about the legs is that they have "tarsi" on the end of them which not only help to attach the legs to the plants they feed from, but also sense or taste sweet liquids that the butterfly might decide to feed on.

The eyes of a butterfly are quite big, and are actually made up of tiny filters called ommatilda, which can sense light, images and movement. Of course, by far the most striking thing about the adult Monarch Butterfly is the wings. There are two front wings and two hind wings. Muscles between the thorax and the wings make the wings move, giving the ability to fly. The wings are not separate entities though – they contain tiny veined tubes which add structure and support. These tubes deliver oxygen and also contain nerves.

Finally, male monarchs have a pair of pincers on the end of the abdomen, which are there to help grasp the female during mating.

The Life-cycle of the Monarch Butterfly

If you're familiar with butterflies in general, you will know that they go through different life stages before they become adults. In fact, they start off their lives looking very different indeed, and only take on the appearance of a butterfly when they reach adulthood. The process is fascinating, and is a good example of the complexity of nature. Several butterflies can be born at once, and will go through the different life stages together, and these groups are called generations. In a single year there can be up to four generations born. Altogether, there are four different stages these creatures go through in order to get their wings.

How long do Monarchs live?

On average, most Monarch Butterflies have an average lifespan of a few months. However, there is evidence to suggest that some of these butterflies can live for several years, depending on their habitat and the conditions in their environment. Most of the time though, it will be different generations migrating every year, rather than the same butterflies. This ability to spontaneously migrate makes their migrations even more impressive!

Life stage: egg

Before laying an egg, the female Monarch has to mate with a male, so that the egg can be fertilised. The male sperm travels through the tiny holes in the top of the egg in order to reach the ovum. Only after this happens will the female be able to lay the egg.

The female Monarch Butterfly only lays one egg at a time, and she will carefully choose the right milkweed leaf to lay on – usually one that is nice and healthy, with no other eggs on it to avoid competition for food. The egg can be found on the underside of the leaf, where it has the most protection from other insects and the elements. Although only one egg is laid at a time, it's important to note that the female is capable of laying up to 500 eggs within a lifetime.

The eggs themselves are very small, so if you're trying to spot them in your garden you may need a magnifying glass! In general they will be about a millimetre or so in diameter, the size of a pinhead. They are white at first, but will usually turn yellowish as the time for hatching approaches. You might also be able to spot ridges or lines running down the egg if you look closely.

About four days after the egg has been laid, it will be ready to hatch into a caterpillar. If you do find an egg in your garden, and you have no idea when it was laid, you can check its progress every day. If it changes colour you will know that it's close to hatching. Don't try to move the egg! Just let nature take its course, and you'll soon see what emerges.

Stage 2: the caterpillar

The egg doesn't hatch so much as get chewed open by the emerging caterpillar. Once it has chewed its way out, the caterpillar will eat the remaining egg shell which is full of important nutrients to help it grow.

The caterpillars go through several changes before they become butter-flies. These stages are marked by the periods between shedding its old skin, which happens five times in the Monarch caterpillar's lifetime.

The first period (or "instar")

When the caterpillar hatches, it will be about 3 millimetres long. These newly formed caterpillars are very tiny and vulnerable, and they will be a duller colour at first, more of a grey than a green. Looking closely you'll see they have black bands on their bodies. Once they have eaten their egg shell they will take a bite of milkweed, the first of many to come! This is not without its risks: sometimes the milkweed can be very sticky and gluey and when this happens, the caterpillar's tiny mouth becomes gummed shut, preventing it from eating. This means that some caterpillars sadly die before they reach the next instar.

Second instar

If the caterpillar survives its first milkweed meal, it will take a break to shed its skin. This brings it to the second instar, when a range of beautiful colours will start to appear on the body, including yellow, black and white. While these colours are emerging, the caterpillar is busy chomping on its next milkweed leaf. However, it's important to note that if you come across a caterpillar that doesn't seem to be eating, but is instead sitting very still, then it may be about to change its skin. Be careful not to disturb the caterpillar at this time, as this is a very important process in its development.

During this instar, the caterpillar will be about a quarter of an inch long. Still small, but considerably larger than when it hatched. It will spend its time eating through 1-2 milkweed leaves.

Third instar

By the third instar, the caterpillar has grown quite a bit. Its striped colouring has become even more striking, so you'll probably be able to spot these caterpillars more easily in your garden than their younger counterparts.

They will be about an inch long, more or less. The tentacles have also grown longer by now and the legs have become more visible.

Fourth instar

During this stage, you'll notice the prolegs (the false legs at the end of the caterpillar's body) are becoming more visible and pronounced. There are five sets of prolegs and during the fourth instar they should have white flecks on them. The filaments or tentacles you see on the front and back of the caterpillar are thicker, blacker and more noticeable by this stage. The caterpillar will eat a huge amount of milkweed to help it grow, and can consume an entire leaf in an hour or so.

Once the caterpillar stops gorging itself on milkweed and stays still, you will know that it is about to shed its skin and enter the fifth, and most eventful, instar.

Fifth instar

By the final stage of its growth, the Monarch caterpillar will be about two inches in length. A long way from its humble beginnings of 3 millimetres! The body will be very plump looking from all that milkweed it has been eating, and you will see that the black bands on the body have an almost velvety look to them, and the surrounding colours are quite vibrant compared to what they were.

Often, the stem of the leaves that the caterpillar is feeding on will break under its weight. This might be a good way to detect the signs of caterpillars in your garden! The fully grown caterpillar, although fattened up, can move pretty quickly. This is because it is searching for a good place to begin its transformation, or pupation, as it is sometimes called.

Once it has found somewhere suitable, most likely a strong, health leaf, it will spin itself a silk pad from which it will hang upside down in the shape of a J in order to shed its final skin. As mentioned earlier, a spiney structure emerges at the end of the body which attaches to the silk pad and keeps the caterpillar's body anchored safely to the leaf. The caterpillar wriggles out of its old skin, and becomes what we call a "pupa" or a chrysalis.

Stage 3: the Pupa

The pupa is a really fascinating structure. It starts off quite soft, but after about an hour its outer shell has hardened, in order to protect the new structures that are mysteriously forming inside. This shell is sometimes called a chrysalis. However, it would be a mistake to call this a cocoon – only moths form a cocoon, which is spun from silk rather than the hard protein shell that the butterfly produces.

The chrysalis is green, which cleverly camouflages it against the leaf and keeps it safe from predators. Inside it, a process called "metamorphosis" (the transformation from caterpillar to butterfly) is underway.

Metamorphosis

During metamorphosis, there are lots of important changes going on. The pupa is literally transforming into another creature inside its green chrysalis. For example, the wings are beginning to form. The mouth is no longer needed to chew leaves and is instead growing into a tube-like tongue that will be able to sip nectar and can be curled up when not in use. Special enzymes are being secreted that will break down all of the caterpillar tissue so that new tissue can grow in its place. New disc shape cells form that will become the basis of the new body parts, for example the wings and legs. The new, longer legs are forming too. These transformational cells are always present in the caterpillar, but they lie dormant until the pupa forms and it is time to replace the old bodily structures with the new ones. This process is nothing short of miraculous, and is unique to insects. It uses up a lot of energy and reduces the body weight of the original caterpillar by half. Waste materials can't be excreted from the chrysalis as it's completely sealed off from the outside world. For this reason, there is often a reddish liquid underneath the butterfly when it first emerges – the waste material it has accumulated during those eventful two weeks.

As time goes on, the pupa will change from a bright green colour to a brownish black. Once the time is near for the butterfly to emerge, you might be able to see the orange and black colours of the wings inside the chrysalis. The butterfly will emerge between 9 and 14 days after it starts the pupa stage.

Stage 4: The Butterfly (adult stage)

Once the metamorphosis has taken place, the butterfly has no reason to remain in the chrysalis. The chrysalis will crack and break open, allowing the butterfly to emerge in all its splendour. If you see a butterfly attempting to emerge from its chrysalis, please don't try to help it along! The process of emerging needs to be done slowly, at the butterfly's own pace. It's thought that the act of struggling out of the chrysalis actually helps the butterfly's development.

Once free from the chrysalis, a built-in instinct tells the Monarch how to use its wings to fly. At first, the wings are wet and delicate, and they appear to be quite small because they've been compacted and confined inside the chrysalis. The butterfly unfolds and moves the wings to dry them out in the air. It is still quite delicate at this stage, and is very vulnerable to predators. During the drying process, a substance called hemolymph is pumped through the veins in the wings and helps to enlarge them to their full size. After about an hour, the butterfly is ready to take its first flight into the big wide world.

Instinct later drives it to find food in the form of nectar, and to eventually migrate if necessary. Adult butterflies typically live for a short time of just two to six weeks (though they have been known to survive for months and even years, depending on environmental conditions). During this time they will be very busy, and not a moment is wasted! From just four to seven days old they are mature enough to mate in order to produce the next generation of Monarchs.

Butterfly generations

We use the collective term "generation" to describe groups of butterflies born at the same time of year. In the Monarch, there are four generations born in total each year.

Although not all Monarchs are born and raised in the Americas, we know that those that have spent the winter in Mexico and the South will emerge in early Spring, around February or March. When this happens, they are emerging from a phase called reproductive diapauses, which is a period when the butterflies cease to mate. During this period, certain hormones stop being produced and the Monarchs will only mate again in February when they are about to migrate back to their summer homes in North America.

Once they have mated, the migratory generation of Monarch females will begin their migration, and when they eventually reach the regions where milkweed grows, they will lay their eggs. Four days later, the first generation of that year's Monarch's will hatch. The juvenile caterpillars will grow for about two weeks before turning into pupae and beginning their metamorphosis inside their chrysalis. After nine to fourteen days, the newly formed butterflies will hatch and they, too, will migrate north. Four to seven days after emerging, these new butterflies will also be able to mate. And they, too, will find a place to lay their eggs during their journeys north. Between March and June, the second generation of Monarchs will hatch and the same life-cycle will repeat again.

In July and August, the third generation of Monarchs hatches. They will grow and transform into butterflies, and will eventually give birth to the final (fourth) generation for that year. The final generation hatches in the early Autumn and has a momentous task ahead: migration for the winter months. Once they reach adulthood they'll embark on their epic journey to Mexico or Southern California where they'll wait out the winter before mating again in spring. These migratory butterflies won't reach sexual maturity that year; instead, they'll go into reproductive diapauses for the next six to eight months – a very long time in butterfly terms! This is a very clever way of ensuring their survival through the winter, rather than laying eggs which would hatch in unfavourable climates and habitats where there is no milkweed to sustain them. Instead of mating, they go into a kind of torpor, similar to a hibernation, which helps them to conserve their energy for the spring.

The Great Migration

The migration of the Monarch butterfly is both impressive and fascinating. However, it's important to remember that only the fourth and final generation of each year will need to migrate. Previous generations will stay where they are and simply die off when the time comes, usually after they have laid their eggs.

The great migration begins in the Autumn, when the temperatures begin to drop. Not all butterflies will migrate to Mexico – their winter destination of choice will depend on where they are coming from, since Monarchs can be found all over North America. However, a large number of Monarchs that were born in the Eastern parts of North America will make for the mountains of central Mexico, to an area called the trans-Mexican volcanic belt. They will have travelled well over 2,000 miles by the time they reach their winter homes – an amazing feat for such small, delicate creatures! On the way, they'll stop to feed on nectar and will also rely on warm air currents which help to propel them, meaning they don't have to use too much of their precious energy reserves. Once they reach Mexico, they will head towards the pine oak forests on the south facing mountain slopes, where they will rest and fall into a state of torpor for the remainder of the winter.

The Mexican forests provide a fantastic micro-climate for the butterflies to live in during the colder months. The mountainous slopes are nearly two miles above sea level, where temperatures can be anything from zero to fifteen degrees Celsius. The forests are humid, which means that the butterflies' wings don't dry out over the winter. The butterflies arrive in their winter homes en masse, which makes for an impressive sight! If you're ever lucky enough to see a migratory group of Monarchs, you can expect there to be tens of thousands of them congregated on a single tree. Sometimes the fragile branches of the pine trees break from supporting so many of these creatures. In general though, they provide the ideal habitat and shelter for the Monarchs. These forests are so important to the survival of the species that the Mexican government has even set up a Monarch Butterfly Biosphere Reserve to preserve their numbers. The cousins of these Mexican migrants, butterflies of the same generation that were born in the Western parts of North America, will spend the winter in California in the same state of semi hibernation. There, they will find a similar micro-climate with Eucalyptus trees, pine trees and cypresses to settle on.

Why do Monarchs migrate?

Like birds, the Monarchs are compelled to migrate in order to find warmer weather over the winter months. In their North American homes, the icy conditions would simply be too cold for the butterflies to survive.

In order to ensure the survival of the Monarchs and their offspring, they must migrate at the first sign of the cold weather arriving. No one knows exactly how they manage to navigate the 2,500 miles to Mexico, but some theories include the earth's magnetic field, and the position of the sun. In 2009, a study was published by the University of Massachusetts Medical School which showed that the butterflies use their antennae to sense light, allowing them to change direction according to the position of the sun. The antennae work in conjunction with the butterfly's brain, both of which have a circadian clock that helps them to tell what time of the day it is. Once darkness falls, the butterflies can no longer fly so they seek out places to roost, usually in trees where there is plenty of shelter. Once the sun rises the following day, they will continue their journey south.

Food is very scarce in the winter months, which is another reason that migration is so essential to the American Monarch's survival. Not only are flowers (the butterfly's source of nectar) very difficult to find, milkweed is also not available as it stops growing in winter. So, even if they were to hatch in such cold conditions, there would be no food source for hungry new caterpillars and they would quickly die.

Lastly, the Monarchs cannot stay in their warm winter homes in Mexico and California for one simple reason: no milkweed grows there. This is why they stay infertile all winter and only begin to mate in spring, when there is time to make it to the milkweed habitat in the north to lay their eggs. These are the reasons why the Monarch has evolved into a migratory species. When you take all of these aspects into account, it's no wonder that these hardy little creatures make such a colossal journey every year!

Why the Monarch is Under Threat

Sadly, today's Monarch Butterfly has come under threat from a variety of environmental issues which have affected its numbers in recent years. In fact, these beautiful creatures have become the focus of conservation efforts by large organisations like the World Wildlife Fund (WWF). In 2014, National Geographic reported that the number of migrating Monarch butterflies reaching Mexico was at an all-time low since records first began in1993.

These figures were based on a report published by the Monarch Butterfly Biosphere reserve in Mexico, where it was found that between 2012 and 2013 there was a 44% drop in the number of hectares covered by Monarchs over the winter. Here are some of the major reasons the Monarch is currently in decline.

Destruction of habitat

One of the major threats facing the Monarch is the destruction of its natural habitat. For the adult Monarch, this threat is to the fields of wild flowers which provide the nectar they rely on for sustenance. Increasing urbanisation is mostly to blame, where land is rapidly being bought up and used for the expansion of housing, offices, car parks and other urban services. What's more, the wild plants and flowers growing in people's gardens are frequently seen as weeds, and the ones which the Monarch would naturally choose to feed off are killed off by pesticides. This scarcity has a knock-on effect in terms of the ecosystem, as the Monarch plays a large role in pollinating the flowers in its habitat.

In their winter homes in Mexico and southern California, there is also a widespread loss of habitat in the form of de-forestation. The Monarchs need these forests in order to roost for the winter and take advantage of the unique micro-climates they provide, using the trees as a form of vital shelter while they rest. Illegal logging has taken its toll on the land, resulting in a deterioration of some of Mexico's (and the Monarch Butterfly's) most precious forest habitats.

Milkweed scarcity

There has been a huge decrease in milkweed in the U.S. in recent decades. This plant is vital to the survival of the Monarch species, since it is the plant of choice for the adult butterflies to lay their eggs on, the leaves of which newly hatched will larvae rely upon for their first meals. Farmers, particularly those with soybean and corn fields, are using more and more pesticides with powerful chemicals that kill plants like milkweed. However, not all milkweed shortages are caused by manmade factors.

Global warming

Freak weather conditions and changes in climate can result in sudden declines in milkweed. For example, a drought in Texas two years ago had a large effect on the migrating Monarchs, most of whom need to pass through Texas in order to reach their winter destinations. This drought meant that a lot of the plants and flowers in the area died off. These flowers and plants would usually provide the necessary sustenance for the Monarchs, which need to build up their energy reserves firstly, so that they can make the journey and, secondly, so that they can sustain themselves over a long winter without food. It's thought that this drought severely impacted the number of Monarch Butterflies that successfully reached Mexico that year, therefore affecting subsequent generations for months to come.

In addition, weather conditions that are inexplicably cold for a certain time of year (the classic signs of global warming) can disrupt the natural migration patterns. Monarchs can run into harsh weather conditions on their journeys south and this can mean they don't survive long enough to reach Mexico. In fact, these climate changes are a huge problem for the animal kingdom in general, not just creatures like the Monarch.

Pesticides

The widespread use of pesticides in modern farming means that there is less and less natural habitat for Monarchs to live, feed and reproduce. Milkweed populations can be easily killed off by these harmful chemicals and in their place, crops and plants that are not of use to the monarch butterfly will be grown instead.

GMO crops

Genetically modified crops such as corn are yet another factor that has influenced the Monarch species in recent years. The pollen of these corn crops contains a toxic substance that kills insects that feed on them. The pollen can also spread to other plants, milkweed for example, in the surrounding area where it kills insects like the Monarch caterpillar. This, of course, has a knock on affect for the following generations of butterflies in terms of their numbers.

Creating the ideal habitat for Monarchs

Now that you know more about the Monarch Butterfly's life cycle and it's habitat, you're probably wondering if there are Monarch butterflies in your garden and if not, how you can attract them. Having these wonderful creatures in your garden will enrich the ecosystem and provide some fantastic opportunities to sit and watch them flit gracefully between your flowers. This section deals with the subject of the garden dwelling Monarch.

Monarch habitats

In general, anywhere that has milkweed has the potential to be a Monarch habitat. Here are some of the more common habitats that can be home to the Monarch:

- Agricultural areas
- Meadows
- Managed green belts
- Conservation areas
- Roadsides
- Gardens
- Parks

Turning your garden into a butterfly habitat

On a very simple level, you could create a butterfly garden simply by providing lots of nectar plants for adult butterflies to feed on as they pass through. However, if you want to provide a sanctuary where the Monarchs can live, breed and grow year after year, then you will need to go one step further by also providing the plants that caterpillars feed on and attach to when the time comes for pupation. So, you'll need to make a strategic decision in terms of the plants that are going to be included in your garden.

What kind of garden do Monarchs like?

The Monarch will favour any garden that is:

- Populated by at least one species of milkweed
- In a sunny spot, with shelter from the wind and rain
- No pesticides or herbicides
- Plenty of nectar plants which bloom at different times throughout the year, so that there is always a food source for adult butterflies

Step 1: Milkweed: the lifeblood of the Monarch

Of course, it goes without saying that the most important thing you could do to attract the monarch Butterfly into your garden is to have plenty of milkweed present. Firstly, the Monarch caterpillar relies on this plant for its first meal and secondly the adult Monarch needs it to lay eggs on. Some species of milkweed can also flower, providing vital nectar for the adult butterflies to feed on. In fact, you might be surprised to know that there are over 100 different species of milkweed! This is not just a common weed, but a very diverse species which you'll need to familiarise yourself with before introducing it to your garden.

Milkweed facts

- Milkweed can be used as a vegetable and produces several types of edible food
- Native Americans used the fibres that milkweed produces for making string and rope
- The downy material produced by milkweed has an insulating effect, and can even be used to stuff quilts and jackets with
- Milkweed is a perennial plant and will appear ever spring in the same locality as the previous year

Buying milkweed

It's important to find out what native milkweed plants are available where you live, and which ones will grow happily in your garden. So, begin by asking at your local garden centre or do a Google search. There are many specialist sites that sell butterfly friendly plants and you might also find seeds being sold on eBay. If you live in the U.S., there is a special milkweed finder tool which you can use here: *http://www.xerces.org/milkweed-seed-finder/*.

When buying milkweed, remember that some garden centres will be wary of using the name "milkweed" because anything with the word "weed" in it can have negative associations for gardeners. They may well be selling it under another name, such as "butterfly plant". The best thing to do is to buy several small plants rather than one large expensive plant. One single milkweed plant is going to do very little to attract Monarchs – you will need several of them to create a real habitat. It's also a good idea to buy a species that will flower, so that you can reap the benefits of also having a plant that feeds the adults with its nectar as well as feeding caterpillars with its leaves.

Gathering seeds

If there is a wild milkweed population near where you live, you could try collecting the seeds and planting them in your garden later on. This is a little bit tricky because you'll need to gather them at the right time – before they have become fluffy. Look for the seed pods that have just recently split, and haven't yet begun to scatter. If you don't wait for the pods to split then it will be too early, and the seeds won't be mature enough. Store the seeds you collect in a brown paper bag, rather than a plastic one to keep them healthy. One important rule for wild seed gathering: make sure you don't accidentally choose something illegal or invasive for your garden. Always thoroughly research what you're going to plant beforehand.

Planting milkweed

Once you have your seeds, the best thing to do is to wait until the Autumn and then scatter them in your desired location. The seeds will lie dormant throughout winter and when the Spring comes and the weather gets warmer, they will start to grow. If any seeds accidentally scatter in the wrong areas of your garden and you end up with a patch of milkweed in the wrong place, you can simply uproot the plants and re-plant them elsewhere.

If timing is a problem (for example if you've left it until late in the season to scatter your seeds) then you can do a clever workaround by cultivating your seeds indoors. All you need to do is trick the seeds into thinking they have gone through a winter. To do this, simply put them on a moist paper towel, and put the towel into a plastic bag. Leave them in your fridge for about a month, checking on them occasionally to make sure no seeds have sprouted early. Once the seeds have been through their fake winter, they will be ready to start growing.

Milkweed life cycle

Milkweed emerges in late spring, when you will see the new shoots popping up from the earth, where the dead stalks of last year's plants were. At first, they might look like small asparagus plants but later they will grow into tall shoots. If you have a species that flowers, then you will see the flower buds appearing in early summer – these look a bit like broccoli heads. Later on in the summer, pointed seed pods will emerge which will eventually become to floss, cotton-like parts you may have seen. Mature milkweed plants can grow as tall as four to seven feet.

Step 2: Add nectar plants

Nectar giving plants are extremely important to the adult Monarch Butterflies, who need a huge amount of energy to complete their annual migrations. Providing a garden that's rich in nectar species will mean that the Monarchs will stop over on their migrations to feed and to breed.

When it comes to providing nectar plants, variety really is the spice of life! Monarchs are much more likely to frequent your garden if you can provide them with a tasty and diverse menu of nectars, which can include both native and exotic flower species depending on your wishes. Here are some important tips:

Regardless of what you choose to plant, be sure that you have species that have a staggered blooming schedule, so that you can provide food over the course of several months rather than just at a specific time during the summer.

Add plenty of colourful flowers to your garden to attract the Monarch. These creatures are able to detect UV light and will naturally be attracted to anything bright. It's a good idea to plant these colours in bunches so that they can be found easily. Reds, oranges, yellows and purples are all popular colours with butterflies.

As well as colour, also think about scent when choosing your nectar plants. A strong, sweet aroma of nectar is likely to attract Monarchs more than a plant with no scent.

Remember to choose the plants that will bloom in the period in which the Monarch is most likely to visit your garden. It's no good investing in a nectar plant only to have it bloom way to early or too late to be enjoyed by your butterflies!

What kind of plants will be attractive to Monarchs?

Rather than relying on hearsay, you will need to be very sure that anything you spend time on planting is actuallygoing to attract Monarchs to your garden.

Here are a few suggestions for what you can plant in the US:

Swamp milkweed (Asclepias incarnata) – this is a useful plant because it has both leaves to feed caterpillars and sweet smelling flowers to feed nectar to the adults

Tropical milkweed (Ascleias curassavica) – another late blooming milkweed that will be very useful in your garden

Mexican Sunflower (Tithonia rotundifolia) – these flowers are very brightly coloured, and easy to grow. They will bloom from mid-summer onwards.

Butterfly Bush (Buddleia davidii) – a perennial bush that can sometimes be invasive, so check carefully before planting.

May Night Salvia (Salvia x sylvestris Mainacht) – this is an early blooming flower that can provide nectar to the first butterflies of the year

Whatever you choose to buy, do your research carefully and get the advice of a reputable garden centre. The plants above are recommended for the US, but if you live somewhere like New Zealand then your choices are likely to be very different, not least because you won't be grappling with the migratory patterns of the North American Monarch.

General tips for Monarch Butterfly gardens

Whether you're a novice gardener or an experienced one, the delicate business of attracting the Monarch butterfly or any butterfly for that matter, into your garden can sometimes be a matter of trial and error. However, if you follow some of these simple tips you should find you're well on our way to a beautiful butterfly haven.

Cultivate tall plants

By growing your plants tall, they are more likely to spread their scents and be spotted more easily by passing butterflies. Like beacons, they will act as little messengers to butterflies in your neighbourhood who will soon realise that there is food to be had in your garden. To do this, you can use trellises, bamboo sticks and other means of support as well as planting flowering vines that will grow up the sides of your garden fence. Some species of milkweed that have tempting flowers will also grow as vines, including Green Milkweed Vine and Honeyvine Milkweed.

Provide both sun and shelter

Butterflies love to bask in the sun, but in the hottest parts of the day they may well seek out shelter in shaded areas. So make sure you have both sunny basking spots as well as shaded areas in your garden. Ideally, your butterfly garden should get around eight hours of sunshine a day which the nectar plants will also need in order to grow.

Use windbreaks

Areas that are sheltered from the wind make the best habitats for butterflies. Fences, walls and thick shrubs can provide this vital shelter, which will entice females to lay their eggs. Butterflies will tend to avoid gardens where there are very strong wind tunnels.

Good soil

Make sure your soil is of the right composition so that the milkweed and nectar plants will thrive. Conditions that can cause issues include overly wet, sandy or clay soils. On the flip side, soil that is too rich can cause fewer flowers to grow, so pay special attention to what you use on your soil. An interesting fact to know is that male Monarchs sometimes need extra helpings of sodium, which they might not be getting from their normal diet of nectar. This sodium helps with their fertility, and it can either be from the soil or from puddles of water. So, providing some open patches of soil and maybe a bird bath or two is a wise idea if you want healthy breeding males in your garden.

Keep plants hydrated

Make sure you give your plants plenty of water over the summer. Plants that dry out will lose their flowers and will no longer be a source of food for your butterflies.

Prune your plants

Get rid of any dead or dying flowers, and new buds will emerge in their places. That way, your butterflies will have plenty of fresh nectar sources. To do this, you can either use pruning shears or you can simply pinch off the flower heads by hand.

Monarch predators

It's important to be mindful of the natural predators to the Monarch – the presence of them in your garden might prove a good explanation as to why you haven't seen the flutter of tiny wings! One thing the Monarch has going for it are its bright colours, both in the butterflies and in their larvae; these colours warn off predators and are a classic sign that an insect is going to be poisonous. However, there are a few predators that can withstand the Monarch's poison, and will still be able to make a meal out of them. Here are some of the most common ones:

Birds

In the winter, some birds have been known to eat adult Monarchs. It's thought that they have less poison in their systems at these times, perhaps because of their long migrations and their semi-dormant phase in the colder months. For birds, food is much more scarce in winter and that means they will try their luck with less appetising insects such as the Monarch.

Wasps

Wasps have been known to attack Monarch caterpillars and sometimes even the adults too. They feed from the abdomens, but in the process they ingest the poison of the monarch and can become infertile as a result.

Spiders

Very occasionally spiders will feed on a small caterpillar if it is caught in their web. In general though, they aren't seen as a huge threat to butterfly numbers.

Ants

Ants have been known to swarm on defenceless caterpillars and feed on them en masse.

Other threats

Fungi, bacteria and viruses can sometimes kill caterpillars, who may be feeding on infected leaves. They can also fall prey to parasites, who lay their eggs on the caterpillar – when the eggs hatch, the young larvae eat and kill the caterpillar.

How to Raise Monarch Butterflies

For the real Monarch enthusiast, there is nothing more exciting than being able to watch these creatures metamorphose into beautiful butterflies. Raising Monarchs can give you the chance to see this amazing feat for yourself. Not only that, it can also help with conservation efforts to improve the numbers of this declining species. Breeding and releasing butterflies into the wild can give their population a boost, and the good thing is that there are no side effects or risks involved in raising them in captivity.

What you will need

You don't need a huge amount of space to rear Monarchs, just a little time and effort. You can buy butterfly rearing kits online and in good garden centres. Because one of the main risks to these butterflies is contamination from fungi and parasites, it's imperative to make sure that all of your equipment is thoroughly sterilised before you use it. In addition, anything that is disinfected needs to be thoroughly rinsed with water afterwards, as these little critters are sensitive to chemicals of all kinds.

29

Keep disinfecting throughout the entire rearing process. Here is a useful list of equipment:

- Disinfectant (wipes or bleach)
- Caterpillar cage (small, large or medium depending on the scale of your efforts, OR you can use a greenhouse setting)
- Butterfly net
- Paper towels
- Tweezers
- Measuring cup for collecting caterpillars, leaves etc.
- Brush for cleaning frass (caterpillar poop)
- Potted milkweed (1 plant for every 2 caterpillars)
- Milkweed cuttings (place these in water, but cover the water to prevent caterpillars falling in!)

Collecting eggs

Once you're ready to rear some monarchs, the first thing to do is go out and collect some eggs. You will find these tiny eggs on the underside of milkweed leaves, if you look carefully in spring time. Once you find them, simply take the leaf on which they are laid and place it in your chosen enclosure.

It's a good idea to keep the eggs isolated from each other until they hatch, in case any of them have picked up parasitic infections. It's also important to remember to label each container with the date the egg was collected so that you can establish its age later on. Once the egg hatches, the fun begins and you can observe it going through the 5 instars of development.

Choosing a container for rearing

It's very important that whatever you choose to rear your baby caterpillars in has enough ventilation. Moisture is bad news for caterpillars and can breed infection. You can either buy a ready-made rearing cage from a specialist shop or website, or you can find a suitable container at home. If it has no air holes in it, you must make some, but they must be tiny enough that the caterpillars can't crawl out of them.

Another alternative is to raise your Monarchs in the safety of a green-house, but in order to do this you must make sure the temperature is properly regulated. The greenhouse must have ventilation, and it must not exceed temperatures of between 70 and 90 degrees Fahrenheit. You will need to provide plenty of shaded areas, air vents and water puddles to keep the butterflies cool.

Looking after your Monarchs

Here are some basic steps for daily care of your growing Monarchs:

- Place your container in an area out of direct sunlight as conditions that are too warm can breed bacteria and dry out leaves.
- Be sure not to keep too many caterpillars in the one container. If you do, you run the risk of the entire population getting sick if just one caterpillar falls ill. Also, you don't want to run the risk of them running out of food because of overcrowding.
- Caterpillars will need fresh milkweed put into their enclosures on a daily basis, ideally twice a day. To do this, you will need to carefully remove the old milkweed and replace it with new leaves.
- They will also need to be cleaned of frass every day, since the build-up of faeces can lead to fungi and infections. A good way to do this is to simply fill the bottom of the enclosure with a paper towel or newspaper, which can be quickly and easily replaced whenever needed. You can use a small paintbrush to remove frass from leaves if necessary.

Feeding your caterpillars

You should only feed your caterpillars the freshest and healthiest milkweed you can find. Never feed them discoloured, dried out or rusty looking leaves. Some Monarch enthusiasts suggest disinfecting your milkweed before giving it to your caterpillars, which is a good way to ensure that no nasty bacteria or fungi reach your baby Monarchs.

If you want to do this, soak the leaves in a disinfectant solution for a few minutes and then rinse them as thoroughly as you can in cold water afterwards. The rinsing part is important or you will end up poisoning the caterpillars.

An alternative to this is growing your milkweed, which can be time consuming but is also a great way to ensure that the milkweed is free from bacteria and parasites. Lastly, if you're going to be keeping your Monarchs in a greenhouse, you'll need to provide both milkweed for your caterpillars and nectar plants for the newly emerged butterflies to feed on.

Caterpillar health

Keep a close eye on your caterpillars for any sign of disease so that you can act quickly if there has been an infection of any sort. Signs that your caterpillars might be ill include:

- A black bodied caterpillar
- Runny poop
- Vomiting
- A strangely elongated body
- Oddly shaped filaments (tentacles)
- An odd or foul smell coming from the container

If you do spot any of the signs above, remove the affected caterpillars immediately and isolate them. Then, remove all the old milkweed and thoroughly wash and disinfect the container, placing the remaining caterpillars safely in a holding container elsewhere until you are finished.

Time to pupate

After two weeks, your caterpillars will have grown plump and will be much bigger than when they first hatched! By this time, they will be ready to pupate, and it is your job to provide them with a safe place to do that.

If you have your caterpillars in a container, the easiest thing to do is simply cover the top of the container with a paper towel or a coffee filter. The caterpillars will be able to safely hang upside down from this surface and pupate. Once the pupa or chrysalis has hardened, you can move them to another enclosure by lifting and moving the paper towel. You must move them to an enclosure where they will have enough room to spread out their wings when they emerge. You can buy online special mesh enclosures for this very purpose. Of course, the ideal thing would be to have moved the caterpillar to its larger enclosure before it has pupated, if possible.

If you notice that the pupa has turned brown or black, then there is a chance that it is unhealthy and it will need to be separated from the rest of your pupae. However, it's important to be cautious because the pupa is going to turn brown anyway just before it hatches. This is because the chrysalis becomes transparent and the brown you see is actually the butterfly inside it.

Adult butterfly

After 9 to 14 days the newly formed butterfly will be ready to emerge from its chrysalis. You will need to just sit back and let this process happen, however long it takes. Don't help the butterfly in any way or you could end up damaging it or hindering its development at this crucial life stage.

These newly emerged butterflies need time to smooth out and dry their wings, and they shouldn't be disturbed for at least 12 hours. After this period, you can either transfer them to a greenhouse enclosure, a butterfly cage or if you like you can release them into the wild. Note that they should only ever be released in warm summer weather when there is plenty of food for them and a favourable climate in which to thrive.

If you choose to keep your new butterflies, they will begin to breed after 4 to 7 days and the fun of raising another generation of Monarchs will begin again!

Fascinating Facts about the Monarch

Here are some interesting things to know about these fascinating creatures.

- Monarch butterflies can't fly if their body temperature is less than 86 degrees Fahrenheit. Instead, they will flap their wings and bask in the sun until they are warm enough.
- Once fully grown, the Monarch caterpillar is a voracious eater and can consume an entire milkweed leaf in 5 minutes. It will increase its body weight by 2,700 times!
- The caterpillars shed their skins 5 times before they pupate.
- The female Monarch is capable of laying up to 250 eggs in one day. In total, females can lay up to 400 eggs.
- Monarch butterflies have a wingspan of around 10cm and weigh just 0.25 to 0.75 grammes
- The Monarch doesn't need camouflage because it's bright colours signify that it's poisonous to predators
- The Monarchs in North America fly up to 6,000 miles per round trip during their migrations each year
- Experts think it takes the butterflies around two months to fly to Mexico each year. In order to travel such a large distance, they take advantage of thermals or warm air drafts, on which they glide in the same way as birds.
- The Monarch can locate and smell nectar with its antennae, and they taste it with the bottoms of their feet!

Conclusions

Now that you know all about the Monarch Butterfly, it's time to see if you can entice some to your garden! Providing these butterflies with a suitable habitat is vital to ensuring their wellbeing and to conserving their numbers for future generations to enjoy. If you care as much as we do about preserving this magnificent species, here are some ways you can help:

Plant some milkweed in your garden

This plant is in decline in rural areas and by planting it in your garden you'll be providing vital habitat for Monarchs to lay their eggs in.

Support the creation of Monarch habitats

Whether it's your local park, school playground, or simply a green road-side area, there is always potential to transform green space into valuable habitats for wildlife like the Monarch butterfly. Plant milkweed and nectar flowers in these areas to support the continuation of the Monarch species.

Lobby against the use of pesticides and GMO crops

Both of these are a threat to the Monarch species and are damaging to the environment in general. If you can come together with your community and lobby against them you will be doing a great service to the Monarch, and to other species under threat from these practices.

Raise awareness

Protect wild flower habitats wherever possible and make sure people in your community know how valuable these wild plants can be.

Help protect forests from logging

The forests of Mexico are under threat from illegal logging and de-foresta-tion. By campaigning against this, you can help protect the valuable winter habitat of the Monarch for years to come.

Thanks for reading! We hope you enjoy having these beautiful creatures basking in your garden, flitting between the plants and sipping nectar from your flowers.

~

www.ingramcontent.com/pod-product-compliance
Lightning Source LLC
Chambersburg PA
CBHW040317010626
45792CB00022B/693